Seasoned

David R. Solheim

North Dakota State University Press
Fargo, North Dakota

North Dakota State Univesity Press
Dept. 2576, PO Box 6050, Fargo, ND 581080-6050
www.ndsupress.org

Seasoned
by David R. Solheim

First Edition

LCCN: 2023943526
ISBN: 978-1-946163-52-3

Cover and Interior design by Nayt Rundquist
Cover images from Pexels by Jesse Zheng and Faik Akmd, used under CC0 license

The publication of Seasoned is made possible by the generous support of the Muriel and Joseph Richardson Fund and other donors to the NDSU Press Fund and the NDSU Press Endowed Fund.

Printed in the United States of America

Names: Solheim, David R., author.
Title: Seasoned / David R. Solheim.
Description: First edition | Fargo, North Dakota : North Dakota State University Press, [2023]
Identifiers: ISBN: 978-1-946163-52-3
Subjects: LCSH: Nature--Poetry. | Aging--Poetry. | Loss (Psychology) | Families--Poetry. | LCGFT: Poetry. | BISAC: POETRY / American / General. | POETRY / Subjects & Themes / Death, Grief, Loss. | POETRY / Subjects & Themes / Family. | POETRY / Subjects & Themes / Animals & Nature.
Classification: LCC: PS3569.O55 S43 2023 | DDC: 811/.54--dc23

Seasoned

Seasoned is dedicated to all my teachers, editors, and writing friends who gave me helpful encouragement over the years, but especially to Rita Johnson of Bismarck High School, Larry Owen of Gustavus Adolphus College, Ken Fields of Stanford University, and Bill Zaranka of the University of Denver, who were the most influential and memorable of my guides.

Contents

Snapshots

Postcards

Four Lost Years

Artistry

Family

Sorting Old Photos

In a shoebox of images once or twice
it happens. An arched eyebrow,
a sideways glance says,
"That's the way he looked,"
"There you are," and the past is present.
The image re-opens entire events.
The last photo of my grandmother returning
from the henhouse, kerchief on her head,
lifting her apron to basket eggs.
The party snap-shot from the night we first made love.

It's like brewing coffee, baking bread,
the scent of lilacs, right here, right now.
Sounds will do it too. My grandfather's funeral hymn,
the oft-repeated tunes from adolescent dating:
"Homeward Bound" and "Tambourine Man."
She is in the mourning of the evening dove
and the call of the lost wild goose.

Sometimes a string of words will do:
how when we were courting,
all night the Northern Lights kept dancing.

Family Anniversaries

In the first month of my adopted children's new lives
I brought them to this wild park.
I have photos of them perched on the cliff.

Thirty years later a grandchild walks the same path
her father trod in childhood. We all pose above
the river carving the valley.

Twenty years before that first visit,
my wife and I unrecognizably young,
her blond hair bandana-wrapped,
me with a bloody knee and torn jeans,
overlooked the same view. Photographed
by friends on the rock ridge now fallen
into the canyon leaving a gap in the past.

The ledge could have been patched in place
and preserved to keep the overlook intact,
but life moves on and we walk
the old territory again, but steps
into memory keep trailing away.

Remembering My Children

Woven on empty branches
winter nests are gray
as barnwood. Inside
straw still fresh as
opened bales.

Farm House

By the wood-burning stove
and kitchen table
bread rises, cards shuffle,
water boils for a galvanized bath.
Homework is written and
butter churns.

Working hands
long gone.

Hello, Darkness

I lean back and rub my spine
against the doorframe,
remember my uncle doing the same,
saying, "Just like a bear against a tree."

I see my ursine kinsmen
circling the pole star,
eat some smoked salmon
before I turn in
for another long sleep,
hoping to wake
in a better world
in a season of light.

July 1936

That morning in his adolescence
my father hitched Ned and Nelly,
his father's favorite team of Belgian bays,
to the mower and headed out to cut
the reeds and sedges
in the dried-out sloughs.

It looked like there would be
no harvest again this year, and
the weedy kochia was already
stacked for winter fodder.

Even the early morning was hot,
and when the shadow of the barn peak
fell straight down for noon,
the trip to the farmhouse
was a welcome break.

In town the CCC boys, who had picked
rocks from plowing all spring and
were building the post office from the stones,
cracked eggs on the sidewalk to cook their lunch.

When the wind rose from the south,
his father said, "That's it." They rounded up
the dozen dairy cows and calves and
drove the herd north to the lake.
The pigs were left with their mud hole
and the chickens the shade of the shelterbelt.

Grandma, the five boys, and
all their livestock were up to their necks
in the middle of Clear Lake,
in the middle of Kidder County,
in the middle of North Dakota,
in the middle of the hottest day ever:
one hundred and twenty-two degrees.

Claim Shack

The farmstead is owned by the neighbors now.
The old house is gone, as was their right.
I took my last walk through my past before
the building was no more. The screen porch
of my father's childhood replaced with a full
living room. The dining room sconces
for kerosene lamps unused for sixty years.
The upstairs bedrooms held sagging beds
under slanted ceilings by the chimney
soot-stained by thunderstorm rains.

The entry shed for the cream separator,
galvanized tub for Saturday baths,
and the hand water pump,
reconfigured with the kitchen.
Windows moved, cupboards
and stoves replaced from wood to coal
to propane gas and indoor plumbing.

During the first remodeling,
when his sons complained the studs
were too far apart for plasterboard panels,
Grandpa said, "I had to stretch a ten-foot budget
to make a twelve-by-twelve shack."
My recollection fills the empty yard
with cedar shingles and red window shutters
while the cellar fieldstones await
the lifting frosts to come.

Guestroom

I am sleeping in my sister's home
on the twentieth anniversary of my wife's death,
in the bed we bought used when we married.

The original black cast iron shows through
the chipped white paint of its present owner
and the antique red of our first décor.

The mattress on the weathered
frame gives this weary body
respite in remembered dreams.

Cross Ranch Folk Fest

In the colorful explosion of early fall
we walked the river bottomland
never out of range of strumming guitars.

I had the seasonal melancholy
of learning of my father's impending
cancer surgery, but little unease about

my wife's knee surgery the next week.
I spent what would be our last date
distracted by my father's likely

leaving of our beautiful time and place.
He would last well into winter, but
she was gone in a month.

Springtime signs are of future
growth and returning birdsong.
Summer of abundant ripeness,

but fall flames out in loss.
More valuable because so brief
and treasured warmth against

winter's empty cold. Remembered
beauty is beauty still and change of season
and change of life roll over and go on.

Last Link

Too slow in answering our phone,
I hear my late wife's voice
promising to call back soon.

I listen carefully once more,
say goodbye again,
pause, and push Erase.

Another Anniversary

Years ago when twenty-one
I wed my high school sweetheart.
Tonight four planets arc in moonlight
across the southern sky as they did
twenty years ago in the wake
of her dying days.

In the adulthood of my second life
entering my own decline
I watch another generation grow
in the inter-planetary glow.

Knotting

For Julia and Daniel
5 March 2016

When I was learning the ropes,
each one had a story.

The groundhog comes out of his hole,
walks around the tree, and
dives back in his hole:
the bowline.

For adjustable tension on a tent rope,
to hold in any kind of weather,
a right hand loop and a lefty
will slide together: two half hitches.

To join two ropes in a bond for equal loads,
one over hand and one underhand wrap
with paired strands on both sides
yields the dependable square knot.
It tightens under equal strain,
but pulling only one line relaxes
its grip and all comes undone.

Two Midwesterners seeking their fortunes
in the big city met at loose ends.

In forming friendship
they raveled from common skeins,
the loss of a parent, life in Seoul,
waiting tables while waiting for more.
Lifelines finding more traction
as each strand braided another.

One spinning vinyl,
one dancing on tiptoe,
they found new music together
bubbling like their laughter.

In early spring they begin
a new tapestry, a complexity
of family and continents,
a fabric like all stories with a dropped stitch
here and there, some mis-matched threads
from different dye lots. This *Once upon a time*
may not end with the magical
They all lived hapily ever after,
but begins weaving music and laughter
and will be beautifully stained by the ripe fruit of love.

New Life

When I was a first grader
my parents bought a brand-new
board game: Scrabble.
Now in my seventies, I play online
with acquaintances in five states.

As the year draws to a close,
I walk the streets of London
and next week Paris in a life
I never dreamed.

After loss I gained another family.
My step-granddaughter hesitates
in her round of good night kisses,
knowing we share no blood
but still are family.

My first family waits in North America
under the same super moon I see here
and the English rain falls
on New Year's Day.

Photo Puzzle

Holiday gathering snapshot
cut into a thousand pieces:
autumn colors and autumn clothing,
blue jeans and dark jackets
standing on asphalt in front of gray trees.
Every piece a shade and variation of the others
until I find a set of eyes. Each fragmented face
reveals the life behind it. Now I see the
personalities of my camouflaged family.

Embers

Nearing a dying hearth
on a chilly day,
he feels the old heat
settling over him,
flushing through limbs
creeping out to fingertips
where he feels
the desire of youth.

Venus

As if cradling a water balloon
he cups his hand to his lover's breast,
brushes her nipple,
and floats on her tides
to a world beyond his grasp.

Vacuum-Packed

I recall you in the office
relishing the aroma of a
freshly opened coffee
package going soft in your hands,
as we lie in bed
in the after-cuddle.

Old Affections

It begins with holding hands,
then caressing locks of hair,
a hand on the shoulder or nape of neck.

Soon lips meet and arms pull together.
The slow dance of legs entwining legs.

Encircling of hips and weaving limbs
pulls lips to ears breathing
words to each other.

Sliding on silk,
friction of flannel,
or cool cotton
we are seasoned together.

After Twenty Years My Wife Calls Me Her First Husband's Name

On an afternoon drive, she turns to me
and says, "Hopkin, let's go home."
A few minutes later, "Did I just call you Hopkin?"
We are startled, but not shocked.
I have been asked about houses where I have never lived.
To remember people I have never met,
to re-call the youth of her children
I know only as adults.

I too have called her another's name.
Asked her to remember things she has never done
in places she has never been.

We are *now* and parts of others' pasts,
and this blurring of lines
is not confusion or failing memory
but the experience of lives harmonized
with the resonance of overtones.

Déjà Vu

As my wife and I doze in easy chairs
before a cozy fire,
I recall finding my parents
in the same condition
when I visited their home
in my own middle age.

As I sipped coffee,
waiting for them to rouse,
I thought that dozing
away at the end of days was it,
not knowing as I do now that
still they dreamed and still they loved.

Experience

Hometown Visitor

The golden arches
lure me from the highway.
Some weed-infested lots
are now a strip mall
featuring yogurt, sunglasses,
and chain-saw sculpture.
The corner gas station
Maggie's Tattoo and Massage
with tanning beds.
First National has torn down
three neglected mansions
and pushes a new façade
of marble and glass
against the edge of downtown.

I pass the houses of friends
gone who knows where.
One house newly-clad in pink shutters,
another's faded green replaced by
brilliant blue. The corner elm
where we used to meet is a
hollowed trunk.

I do not recognize the van
in the driveway of my old home,
but in the twilight I see a child's
bicycle leaning against the brick planter.
The yellow light from several rooms
comforts me like a winter hearth
as I drive off into the arms
of encircling darkness.

Home at Dusk

In the long grass in the ditch
two glowing eyes blink
and fly off in different directions.

I am startled back to childhood
campouts when lightning bugs
dotted the night like shooting stars.

They flash their mating code
like my remembered dreams:
phosphorescence floating,

luminescence on the windshield,
evening star on the western horizon.
I drift among the flickering flames.

Savannah

My neighbors and I
thin the woods
between our homes
and cornfield.

We no longer swing
from limb to limb, but
like the first two-legged walkers
we claim the scattered trees
to break the horizon,
shadow heat,
drift blizzards,
and nest birdsong
come spring.

Fire Flies

In the heat of July, evenings
welcome lightning bugs
flash attractive
codes of organic light.

In childhood, jars of them
lit our camp-out tents
for reading stories of
far-flung adventures.

Like Fourth of July fireworks,
they explode the night and
settle on dark soil
returning to larval life.

Now one pulses light
in the palm of my hand
and more rise up into swirling
galaxies minute as earth in space.

On the Edge of Town

I sit on my patio in the waning light
trying to finish the Sunday crossword.
Blue jays complain about the empty feeder,
turkeys peck through the brush,
and a nighthawk screeches over yellowing corn.
A humming bird zips out of the dusk,
hovers near my ear, then in front of my face.
The green iridescence cocks its head
from side to side eyeing me, the bird-watcher.
Satisfied this red-shirted being offers
neither nectar nor danger,
it buzzes away drawing
last light into the woods.

Great Blue

Herons flap off grumbling
when my kayak nears.
Lilies open their floating worlds.

I walk among the buzzing
wild flowers, and butterflies
wing by like orioles.

The nighthawk begins his
rasping dives over the
neighbor's cornfield.

Lightning bugs dance
and I fly in the meteor
shower of midnight sky.

July Fourth

All night my skylight
flickers like a neon sign.
Clouds rumble like
coal trains to a power plant.
Indifferent Nature's downpour
celebrates its independence.

Mid-Summer, Late In Life

Three chickadees murmur
in the hawthorn.
Two nuthatches assume
their topsy-turvy view of the world
on the pine tree trunk.

A speckled robin lies in the brush
and the hollyhocks have been
pulled into oblivion by voles.
Daisies and poppies
beheaded by gophers,
I enjoy all survivors: iris,
echinacea, and prairie smoke.

I await the budding milkweed
and late sunflowers.
Review grandchildren's photos
and scatter winter
ashes across seedbeds.

Just Before Dusk

After two weeks of looking
at bird poop on my window,
I go outside and wash it clean.

Lightning bugs start courting,
and from a mile away a cotton
wood seed drifts into the grass.

Food for a chipping sparrow
or to begin a sapling, it makes
no difference to the seed

or the watcher
behind the window
waiting to see the stars.

Outrider

Eight geese wedge their way
to the western fields, and
a ninth straggler closes
the gap between itself and the convoy.

Sets its wings and sails over the skein
which shifts below it, and flies along
double-spaced from the flock,
continuing the conversation.

But distanced from
the tight formation, it
remains unpaired and
on the fringe of order.

Sunday Evening

As I wheel the trash bin to the curb,
fireflies flare like shooting stars and
lift my vision above shadows where
the moon rises and three planets glow.

In distant space a nebula explodes,
a galaxy disappears, and somewhere
something thinks, "How beautiful.
Just like a lightning bug."

In morning, my walk
is littered with insect husks.

Summer Ends

Loons yodel
the misty morning.
Like raindrops,
warblers rustle leaves.
Red-capped sparrows
pick through clover.

In my lawn chair,
I sip my coffee and
begin another autumn
not going off to school.
The woodpecker taps
a hollow tree.

Fire Season

The landscape ochre-tinged
sumac leaves, husks of corn,
rusty bunch-grass
all frost bitten.

The setting sun,
a blood moon.

Late Harvest

In this dry season
the rooted world
eases toward sleep.

In the woods, birch and
cottonwood blaze yellow,
sumac and maple bleed.

Each breeze
is dappled with
drifting leaves.

In prairie fields
cobs bow with gravity
on faded maize stalks.

Even at night
machines crawl
in pools of dusty light
before snowfall.

IED

Returning from a quick trip
to the grocery store,
I take the leisurely route
around campus.

On the back-road access,
I see what looks like
a wad of Christmas wrap,
straddle it with auto chassis,

and as I pass over it
in an instant I imagine
what I have done
in the Tigris basin.

Snow Day

In the winter of super moons
now in my eighth decade,
I prepare for beginning another year.

Like the night of my birth, so I was told,
snow piles up on roads and fields.
Traffic is light and animals are busy.
A coyote prowls the edge of town,
woodpecker's rapping is muffled
in wind-borne flakes and finches
blaze red around sunflower feeders.

When I graduated from college, men
first walked on the moon. This new year
hosted a super full moon. My birth month
will close with a blue moon eclipse.

If my first words were, "My moon,"
I give up my claim, happy to share
the darkness-ending light.

Blood Moon

The trees are stripped to their bones.
Geese squabble in the corn stubble.
One squirrel buries nuts, another digs them up.
The cattle huddled in pens, a drover with a whip
smokes a cigarette by the slaughter-house door.
Two murderous crows finish butchering a finch.
The eagle's abandoned nest is reflected
in the skin of ice on the swamp
underneath this light.

Negatives

In mid-winter snows
the blond squirrels
chase the gray ones
into danger,
freezing when the hawk
circles overhead.
Not like autumn
when russet protects and white
catches the predator's eye.

Spring Snow

Canadian geese pace in the
cornfield beyond my yard,
ruffle their feathers, and
settle on black earth.
The snow falls.

Blue jays and cardinal
bedecked for spring but
trailing winter, grab
seeds from the feeder.
The snow falls.

Red wing singers from
cat-tailed swamps,
too-early arrivals,
trill in the firs.
The snow falls.

Regular customers,
chickadees, juncos,
purple finches, and I
go about our business.
The snow falls.

Spring Fed

This week the coulees run knee-deep
filling stock ponds against summer heat.
Prairie river flows bank full, and melting
snow banks promise green.

After seventy seasons of random loss,
my hope springs again, amid calls
of northbound cranes and
ripples of running water.

Respite

When the social world is chaos
I recall the solitude of blizzards,
the isolation of blocked roads,
heightened silence of snowfall,
and emanations of drifting
light in evening solace
from the fractured days.

Over the Bar

When I was a school high jumper,
the local paper printed
a photo of fans watching me
attempt a leap. In it I see
girls in other guys' letter jackets
squeeze notebooks against their breasts.
Boys and old men stand on one foot
leaning back to help lift my trailing leg
while the fiberglass barrier wobbles
on the standard, marking my passing.

School Reunion

Women I longed to fondle
fifty years ago, embrace me
with spontaneous affection.

After long separations,
we luxuriate in light
this blue moon.

A Clean, Well-Lighted Place

Classmates fifty years ago,
four old friends meet again for lunch.
English majors then, readers and writers all,
they greet each other entering
their eighth decades.
Their paths crossing again
from youth to age, their talk is now:
this week's movie, recent reading,
camping trips, long walks, and river journeys
from smiling lips and gray heads
bobbing in a circle of winter sunlight.

Gifted

My classmate who lived in his car
while selling pots and pans
for months after graduation
hands me yet another book,
saddle-stitched letter-press,
"It's a re-telling of folklore,
You might enjoy it."
Now retired in his suburban home,
he says, "I'm trying to get
all my belongings into a backpack.

When I sell the house, I'll be free."
After collecting for years, my friends and I
want to pile everything on the corner
for someone else and walk away.

For JT at Thirty and Seventy

—John Thomas Maluski 1945–2021

I.
It's a short trip
from Steele to Bismarck.
You must have made a wrong turn
to get there so late in life.

It wasn't like those early journeys,
a Saturday round trip on Greyhound or the old NP.
You spent your nickels for dime store rings
and a quarter for the smell of onions
at Jack Lyons Hamburger Stand.

Nor are your friends those slim-hipped ones
whose slippery pants you sent crashing to the classroom floor.
None of us any longer spend
a week's wages on a weekend's drinking.
The spirit is willing, but the flesh is weak.

In olive drab you spent those long
days of lab research with the racing forum.
After discharge you charge around the Fargo
winters in that frozen pick-up truck,
no longer alone, but still some cold times
despite the fury to keep warm.

Now approaching mid-life, on the ice
you plod from hole to hole to measure
the depth of Sweetbriar, to set your
line for your fishing spot.

Tonight you measure us and find
your place is here. In January,
we make for you and yours
a place within us safe and warm.

II.
Now both of us friends of Bill,
we are in new lives with new wives.
The coastal waters lap your toes
and off across the wide Pacific
you taught English in Asia,
escaped a tsunami and raised a second son.

I recall our long nights of poker games,
trivia drinking games, chilly days
hunting wild birds, drinking coffee
in a warm car patrolling gravel roads.

Our occasional holiday meetings, not
lost in the past, but pushing our presents
into our futures. Our lives woven like
shelterbelts on prairie farms and tangled
old fences that cross in the middle of nowhere.

In the midlands I take my daily walk
and feed the birds you taught me to see
while you practice tai-chi
in the Salem park. Both of us discovering
like Simon and Garfield's old friends,
"How very strange to be seventy."

Again in bleak mid-winter, we find
warmth in our memories and dream
of future times together in spirit and fact
no matter how long since we have met,
no matter how far apart.

Phantom

Another old friend has left me behind.
My day filled with holes of former habit.

No cans to open, no chin to scratch,
no vibration on my chest
soothing me to a midday nap.

I imagine other friends gone home
and hear the mewling of someone
about to enter the world of sleep,
or about to leave it.

Lost

I have reached the age when my friends
are assembling in cemeteries.
The dated stones suggest finished stories
even though I know they only stopped.
I have the comfort of shared times
and expect no further installments.

It's my missing friends I wonder about.
They are like stories I want to finish reading,
disconnected phone lines, bounced emails,
letters stamped "Unknown at this address,"
the single tennis shoe I pass
on the shoulder of the highway.

Leaving

I clasp my friend of years,
who might not know me
when next I call.

I admire his patient
noting of hunting locations,
recitation from old books,

and the thinning of our friends.
I think of my own drifting away
and midnight recollections.

The photos on the walls of memory
depict us as we are inside, but
show our bodies' continuing betrayal.

Seventy

Traversing my old campus
I realize this is not what I remember.

Old friends and feelings are long gone.
Ignoring the transparent shell of January,
I slip, stagger, and teeter on one foot,
then resume my walk listening
to the January thaw running
in the veins of the street.

I gather my census
of old friends and
think of the waters
under the snow.

Prescient

Day by day my body leaves me.
It creaks and lumbers around the house
bumping into furniture, stubbing its toes.
Struggling to open pill bottles,
dropping crumbs on its chest.
I grieve my separation
from this old friend of my youth.

Even in its better days gangly and awkward,
all elbows and knees, a friend remarked.
Though lithe enough to hurdle
and fast for a quarter mile.
Its vision and hearing still clear,
it continues to shepherd me
around in this world.

Brown Study

Roll top desk, recliner, bookshelves of poetry,
paintings by a dead friend, family photographs,
several bison images, prairie grasses,
an aerial shot of grandfather's homestead,
and a couple of plaques from teaching days.

This is my abode, and I seldom visit
the other rooms for food or sleep.
The study's twin vertical windows
become French doors opening into
the garden of another life.

Rite of Passage

When I am done with breathing, scatter
my ashes across the wide Missouri.
From Fort Mandan or Double Ditch or
Burnt Boat Creek, and I'll depart
the heart of North America
to enter eternity.

The *Far West* will paddle-wheel
my cremains from sandbar to sandbar
down the Mighty Mo.
Drifting from island to island
in the Father of Waters,
I'll inch my way to the Gulf,
the saltwater mother of all, and
re-enter the cradle endlessly rocking.

Snapshots

North Country

I'm from silence
where little is said
and nothing
is said twice.

Late Thaw

The countryside wears
the mottled skin of age
or acned adolescence
belying adulthood
coiled below the surface.

Peepers

The rain-freshened pond
awakened frog-song for mates.
Herons' dinner bells.

Before Seedtime

I see garden bells
waving, but wind dances sound
silently away.

Spring Break

Corn and beans sowed, each
farmstead an emerald isle
floating on black seas.

Evening on the Lake

Egrets and pelicans glow
in one beak a fish shimmers.

Interdependence Day

July dusk spangled
by fireflies lighting backyard
fir like Christmas Eve.

On the Horizon

Clouds shower onto earth
rivers stream into sky.

Cat Nap

In my after lunch
ease she curls in my lap weaves
me into her dreams.

After Eden

Leaves scattered
we see Nature's bones
not its green gown.

Eyeing

The ripened bluestem,
the rusty hawk hunts
from the russet oak
feathers frosted leaves.

Swinger of Milkweed

After Robert Frost

A squirrel climbs the stalk
nearing the seed pod
as it bends back to earth.

It releases its grasp,
seeds flying out
toward the heavens.

Caw

Dying elm's
leafless crown
blossoms crows.

Country Graveyard

From their white boxes
the bees make honey
not in the lion's head,
but among the dead.

Buffalo Gap

A wind-blown juniper
atop a butte
the pennant on
the circus bigtop.

Against Darkness

A combine in a cornfield
pours gold into a truck box
seeding the silos of January
with sunshine.

Solstice Moon

Shines on skeletal birch
scattered among cedars
before snowfall
buries all.

Mid-Winter Eve

Beyond my kitchen window
magnolias have wrapped
their flower buds in fur.

Even as the wolf moon rises,
willow catkins test the air
beside the frozen swamp.

Birthnight

The red-bannered bird
bobbing at the suet feeder
began my celebration.

By evening Mars smoked red
and waxing moon and
crystal dippers circled Polaris.

Leaving the stellar bears
aloft in ice, Orion
stalked the southern skies.

What Cheer

Cardinal from
snow-shrouded spruce
sings spring.

Postcards

Mirage

Nevada towns glow all night
flashing exotic names:
Araby, Xanadu, and Shangri-la.
Come to the oasis tonight.
We may be gone tomorrow
taking with us all your chances.

Near Buffalo, Wyoming

Scattered in the median
of the interstate junction
rusty, black lava boulders.

In twilight
shaggy beasts
gather again.

Wild West

A leafless cottonwood
leans over a dry creekbed.

Boas

Scaled tire treads
litter the roadside
shed skins of fossil
fuel constrictors.

Self-Portrait in a Convex Tanker

The dairy trailer reflects
the road and circling sky
as following traffic disappears
into the center of the mirror.

My sedan stretches to limo length and
passes its momentary reflection.
The dotted lines pulsing,
the transport continues on its milky way.

Response

The curved hunk of tire tread
transforms into a turkey
with a clutch of chicks extending
her tail into my lane.

The seventh chick crouches
in the seam of the shoulder
then darts into the ditch
as I inch past.

On the hillside a farmer pauses
his swather while a pheasant
and her brood scurry away
from its flashing blades.

We continue our rounds pleased
we haven't wasted our lives today.

Upland Game Season

Young men roam the countryside.
Armed, they must shoot something.
A tin can, an empty farmhouse,
birds on the wing, or an angry face.

Old hunters stalk the margins
of woods and field pausing
in no hurry to fire knowing
they have only a few rounds left.

Two Story Family

On the upper level, the old widow
continues her daily tasks:
washing dishes, ironing clothes,
and afternoons dozing over her scrapbooks
where her grandchildren will find her life.

On the ground floor, the middle-aged couple
pay bills, drive off to work, and,
after dinner, listen for
the mouse-like scurrying overhead.

Last Hunt

The octogenarian stands
agape at the four-wire fence
knowing he can't lift either
knee high enough to straddle it.

Never imagining today,
he recalls being a hired hand
leaping such fences
toting a sledgehammer.

On the other side,
his spaniel whines
and pheasants cackle
in the distant draw.

Flowering Shrubs

Red bud, lilac, apple, and plum
float like mist above greenness
wafting haze promising
fruit beyond the horizon.

Crossing Southland

Longhorns graze bayous
where egrets ride
their motley hides.
Water lilies and magnolias
begin to bloom.
Live oaks shrouded
in Spanish moss,
the end of empires.

Kudzu

Vines wrap trees into
temple spires of forgotten
cities, faiths outgrown.

Retiree

Floating in a suburban pool,
I see the vulture circling and
in the distance military contrails
again scar my sky.

Island Retreat

Thump, thump, thump at eight AM.
Axe and mattock of the day laborer
thinning the woods next door
awakens me in the rented house.

On my morning walk,
I see another worker raking
the flotsam sea grass
from a private beach.

I stroll in summery sun, and,
remembering those workers,
after my fish dinner, I leave
my waitress an excessive tip.

Brain Coral

After three nights of sinusitis
on my tropical vacation,
I dream I'm smoking a pack a day again,
recall Egyptians thought it
a mucous-producing organ
removed through the nostrils
for mummification.

Beach Comber

Low tide strands the best:
clamshells and coral,
crab claws and conch.

High tide grinds it all
to sand and rolls in
fresh detritus.

Underwater ripples of sand,
foam of wavelets, and
flashes of sunlight

dizzy my steps.
Eyes on my feet,
tomorrow I'll search again.

Tonight I dream
pieces of eight.

Summer People

In the October drizzle
on the dappled hillsides
in seasonal cabins, folks
burn their last firewood.
Smoke settles over our brown valley
where we harvest apples and pumpkins and
trim pine boughs to decorate their urban holidays.

Rock Creek Lodge

As the evening bear paws through
the fire-scarred mountainside
meandering across and down,
he doesn't know he is watched
by a tourist on the creek-side deck,
who doesn't know why the shadow
pauses by a white boulder,
disappears in a copse of brush,
or where he will spend the night.

Winter in the Pacific Northwest

Beyond my morning mug
yellow slickers,
wet dogs, and
moss-encrusted vagabonds.

Polar Vortex

As its molecules compact,
the air itself presses like a glacier.
Houses creak,
bones ache, and
trees explode
in its grasp.

Like mammoths on the tundra
in the last ice age,
we are preserved
by its embrace.

Four Lost Years

Civility

Larry Leventhal 1941–2017

As the forty-fifth president raises
his right hand for his swearing in,

the cantor begins the funeral for
the civil liberties lawyer of my youth.
The rabbi tells us "Judaism is about memory.
Memory is where Larry now lives."
The woman next to me nods in her hijab,
as does the row of yarmulkes in front of us.

The gathering is full of three-piece suits,
his colleagues, I suppose, but scattered throughout
black faces, jeans, boots, and feathered decoration.
The guitarist sings a ballad composed for this day,
the family recounts its joys and losses with this life.
The American Indian Movement client speaks of this brother
from Wounded Knee and master of treaty rights,
promises never to be arrested again, on Christmas Eve,
shakes his rattle and chants his honor song.

I am the least of these, a client for a day, but belong
to the circle of all he helped. The rabbi continues,
"Now is the time to say goodbye."
Then three Ojibwe pulse their drums
and trill as if all our hundred voices were in them.
No American Carnage here, just another
life seeking justice for others.

Hay Creek Manifesto

The essential American soul is hard, isolate, stoic, and a killer.
—D. H. Lawrence

In my grade-school years my friends and I
hiked over the hill beyond city limits
exploring the countryside down to the creek.
Sometimes we carried our rods and reels
and wet our hooks in the fishless ponds.
Sometimes armed with bows, we hunted
gophers and speared crawfish in the creek.
With our shouldered BB guns we paraded
for target practice in a wooded draw.
Once we killed a shrike and convinced ourselves
that killing a butcherbird was not as bad
as shooting a robin or wild canary.
That day devolved into air rifle war,
three against three, but the first few hits
caused a hasty truce. We marched
back home warily eying each other.

On our last hike in junior high, walking
the railroad line in the valley as we
exchanged hearsay about sex and violence,
a Clint Eastwood type came out of his shack
a quarter mile away, shook his fist at us,
and sent a bullet whizzing overhead.
We dodged down the embankment
and kept low profiles all the way home
wondering who was in the wrong.

Now the self-righteous arm the aggrieved,
whose lethal lessons ricochet down halls
and make classroom massacres
against imagined oppressions
the final point the gunner's self-demise.

From a throne of guns and ammo
an automaton stalks us all, seeks
the thrill of power delivered from a distance
drags us off to Sandy Hook and Columbine,
sends from Florida a bloody Valentine.

Zero Tolerance

A bored third-grader, my granddaughter
twists herself into the kennel, latching its door.
Pleased with her trick she smiles through wire mesh.
I snap her picture. She growls, I snap again.

I carry her trapped around the kitchen.
She snarls and hisses, then purrs
like the pampered pet she is.
Placed back on the floor, she frees herself.

Telling her mother about the child's day,
I show her the photos. She winces. "I know
it was only play, but I can't stand,
even for a moment, to see her caged."

We hold this image of our child
like the thousands caught in the net.

Marginal

The ebbing tide leaves scattered shells,
sand dollars, twisted kelp, and charred logs.
Cormorants dive beneath the breakers
and gulls inspect the sea foam.

Inland, deer and elk browse meadows,
wolves eye from forest edge,
and bears merge with shadow.
Memory dawns from savannahs.

Genius endures in detention camps,
where would-be writers seek paper scraps,
and children rub charcoal designs on walls.
Tectonic plates grind each other.

The spaces between these inky words rumble.
Like lightning imagination strikes.

American Family

When I was a child,
all my relatives were pure
Norwegian-American Lutherans,
though one ancestor was rumored
to have been part Swede.

We played sandlot baseball
with Catholics, had one or two
Lakota kids in grade school classes,
and patronized shops owned by Jews.
My farming uncles had "Rooshan" neighbors,
and our little city had its lonely Black man
who farmed with horses on the edge of town.

In adolescence I learned a family member
had married a Catholic, divorces had fractured
family unity, some didn't go to church.
some drank too much, and at least one cousin
did time in prison. Most continued marrying,
begetting, adopting, and re-marrying.

In maturity my family has Asians and Blacks,
Hispanics, Jews, and Native Americans.
Some are gay. Who knows what
church, if any, one might attend?
Far from perfect, none of us will be
chiseled in stone or etched on coins,
but we are now linked within
the circle of all our relations.

In the Middle

Middle class, midwestern, middle-aged,
I muddle along. Not noted for gender
or ethnicity, I background the majority.

Probably passed over for a job or two
or even a late promotion, I live
in a comfortable neighborhood.

My neighbors wave and nod when
I walk the street. I come and go
as I please, day or night.

They think I'm one of them,
and I am outside. But if they knew
my heart, they'd turn on me

as if I were the other they fear.
We who hate what's been done
to the world to keep us in line.

Neglect of children, low wages for profits,
military order, disease on the rise for
those who look different or disagree.

Under Siege

Repeatedly I wake at four AM
and pace my outpost
in the widespread war.

Our own forces are draining the moat
and undermining the walls. The monarch
sends his minions hither and yon at whimsy.

Citizens grow restless, ready to throw the old
over the ramparts to appease the enemy.
Some hurl cobblestones against authority.

I ascend the watchtower, scanning
the smoking horizon, while danger
stirs in dungeon and castle keep.

Public Enemy

Some rob you with a six-gun,
Some with a fountain pen.
—Woody Guthrie

While my father stood in line to buy stamps,
I examined the faces on the post office
wanted wall dreaming how I would spend
the rewards for the gunmen and mobsters
whose photos the FBI had posted there.

Now I see low-caliber number forty-five
running resorts for tax-spending guests,
secret service agents and foreign dignitaries,
like P. T. Barnum needing a sucker every minute.

Making perfect phone calls: wanting
a favor though; begging the auditor
to recalculate for ten thousand votes
plus one to fake his win.

He rallied the badly educated. They stormed
the Capitol. His avatar put his booted feet
on the Speaker's desk and stole her mail.
At the Senate dais prowled a manimal,
a tattooed lost boy from Neverland.

Forty-five tweeted his pseudo-reality show but
wouldn't accept his own catch-phrase,
"You're fired." He vacated the White House,
packing gold-plated plumbing and light bulbs.

His epiphany: the post office bulletin board
is the only place where he is Most Wanted.

Vaccine-Enabled Road Trip

In the hillside field above
a blue banner with the
former president's name in white
and his red MAGA slogan
stretched between two
green porta-potties,
workers on hands and knees
plant walla-wallas and vidalias
bound for my dinner table.

Unaccompanied Minors

One April day, my pre-teen children-to-be
somehow said good-bye to their birth-mother,
boarded a plane in Seoul, and jetted into the day before
to begin their futures across the Pacific.

Two landings later, we met them in mid-America
each of us knowing only a few mutual words:
cake and ice cream, bathroom, and welcome.
And drove a couple more hours to their new home.

Our prairie village helped raise them.
We found a Korean speaker for family meetings,
one friend who taught ESL, a counselor down the block,
and an emergency room for the first bicycle accident.

We also saw the looks and heard some words
I won't repeat. In the annual school photos
black-haired islands among a sea of blonds.
Long struggles with the irregularity of "stupid English."

Now both are health-care professionals raising
their own children through childhoods they never had:
sharing kimchi and bulgogi, pancakes and roast turkey.
Singing the ABCs and "All the Pretty Little Horses."

Dreaming back through our years, I imagine the parting.
A single-mom waitress/bartender beset by all woes
from Pandora's box, finds at its bottom Hope
and sends her children off to a land with opportunity.

Every day, across borders, behind walls,
other mothers sigh and begin walking
their children down the early road
into the unknown, off to living other lives.

Artistry

Folk Art

Thirty years ago on the high moraine
a farmer looked at a pile of plowshares
and thought, "I could make something out of that."

He arranged them across the shop floor,
welded the outline of his horse, and
mounted it in the roadside pasture.

Startled by the transparent being, passersby
pulled in and made requests: sheaves of wheat
for the grandson of the bonanza farm,

the wildlife club called for pheasants and geese,
a nearby town "Welcome" with grain elevators,
a Hereford's head to support the neighbor's mailbox.

His images from the scrapheap of farming
enlivened fifty miles of roadside.
Today they've rusted into sod.

Different names collect mail and tires painted
"No Hunting" hang from gateposts. Some of us
remember the artisan's hand and see it still.

With this breath and while these pages last
the art survives the artist, though these too
are destined to dusty death.

Re-Sources

I'm from open country and
towns that still have edges.
Rivers that carry the heart
to places where other people live.
Where clouds roll over
like waves of fear and
ideas strike like lightning.

Craftsmen

As I write in my study,
workmen across the street
erect a house.
Studs and rafters frame
open space,
locking in privacy.

The stuff of my poem
exists in the solitude
of memory and imagination.
I shape some windows
open to light and voyeurs.
Enticing doors
lure the curious
and capture them.

Hobby Farmer

My silo full of books,
I load up a couple dozen,
head to the local
Poetry Farmers' Market,

intone some free samples
at the open mic,
buy two books from my fellow readers,
and head back to my table.

When the market closes,
I've sold a handful of books and
pocket some folding money.
Next week the County Fair.

Scrap Iron

In the leafless shelterbelt
along the gravel road,
old machinery rusts away
like writer's drafts
and discarded lines.

Child's Play

Before I knew the taste of peaches,
I remember finding their pits
left behind by scratching chickens
in the ash heap of the burn barrel.

These stones more intricate than
medicine bottles and broken dishes.
The furrowed shells like petrified brains
wound around some secret knowledge.

I arranged shards in imaginary towns
peopled by peach seeds. Little minds
like my own wrinkled hemispheres
coiled around the germs of trees.

In the British Museum

So many shapes and textures here.
The fluted arches of gothic cathedral,
cobblestone of Roman roads,
Egyptian sarcophagi embossed
with hieroglyphics as if carved last week.
A giant scarab entranced as soapstone essence.

In ancient marbles
the sacrificial bull still
bellows at the sky,
the fur and muscles of his neck
soft as diaphanous
robes floating on attending maidens.

It is all we tourists can do
to caress with only our eyes.

Art Song

I glimpsed the poet as a child
in her father's, my professor's, home.
She chats about her elegiac poems:
ironing, combing her mother's hair,
both their hands on the keyboard,
sandbar parties, and musical motifs.

The piano sounds. Her daughter's voice
fills the room then trills and dances,
chants of daily tasks. In overtones
I hear my late wife's voice
now gone for twenty years.
Under it all, the river flows.

I want to hold the poet's grief,
forestall the losses to come.

August from My Desk

After Roland Flint

Sumac hints at red
black-eyed Susans close
maples flare in five fiery tongues
hawthorn ripens.

A triple horse team
rakes a windrow
and dust from
my father's youth

settles on my car.
The bays plod along
circling the shrinking field,
yet the horseman dreams

of someone like me passing
him on state highway three.

Hibernation

The bear dens up
for her winter slumber.
When she wakens,
she is a mother.
Two cubs are there.

In these darkest days,
I drift into dreams of poems.
When I awake
in the morning light
there they are.

Dream Limerick

The widow's young grief was well known
by the tears on her cheeks and her moans,
but down deep inside
she knew she had died
and her body would live on alone.

Driving Home Late from a Robert Bly Reading

It is a cold and snowy night.
Traffic is light on route one-sixty-nine.
Snow fills my headlights like supernova nebulae.
Approaching cars are glowing igloos on ice floes.
The streetlight marks my house with a tipi of falling snow.
I park in the drive and idle.

Another Road Trip

Passing the places of memory:
my grandparents' homestead,
ghosted by bison and Lakota;
the attic from dusty childhood
in a steamboat river town;
a multi-tiered osprey nest;
a wind-blown claim shack
with scattered chimney bricks
holding shingles on the roof;
I see they are not as I described them.

They exist in time and solid space
not in language or imagination,
yet all these words of mine are true.

Index of Titles and First Lines

Acknowledgments

The following periodicals first published the listed poems.

Humanities North Dakota Magazine: "Folk Art"
Mankato Poetry Walk/Ride: "Great Blue," "Before Seedtime" & "Scrap Iron"
Meat for Tea: The Valley Review: "Civility," "Zero Tolerance," "Hay Creek Manifesto," "Marginal," "Boas," "Two Story Family," "Phantom," "American Family," "Another Road Trip," "Hobby Farmer," "Under Siege," "Hello, Darkness," "Dream Limerick," "Public Enemy," "Mid-summer, Late in Life," "Knotting," "Sorting Old Photos," "Just Before Dusk," "Birth Night," "Savannah," "Fire Flies," "Snow Day" & "Rock Creek Lodge"
North Dakota Quarterly: "Hometown Visitor," "Remembering My Children," "Polar Vortex," "Buffalo Gap," "Guest Room," "North Country," "Rite of Passage" & "Lost"
On the Seawall: a community gallery of new writing, art, and commentary: "August from My Desk" & "Unaccompanied Minors"
On Second Thought: "Home at Dusk"
Pembroke Magazine: "Over the Bar" & "Mid-winter Eve"

About the Author

David R. Solheim, the North Dakota Statehood Centennial Poet, has published writing in more than two dozen periodicals and had work in several anthologies. He wrote two poetry chapbooks published by Dacotah Territory. His four previous books of poetry and a literary travelog related to Thoreau's 1861 visit to Minnesota are available via buffalocommonspress.com. Solheim is an English Professor Emeritus of Dickinson State University, where he taught for almost 30 years, and, thanks to the late Larry Woiwode, an Emeritus Associate Poet Laureate of North Dakota. He holds degrees in English and creative writing from Gustavus Adolphus College, Stanford University, and the University of Denver. Early in his career, he was a temporary faculty member at NDSU, and conducted numerous programs for the North Dakota Humanities Council (now Humanities North Dakota) and the ND Council on the Arts. After residing in Minnesota for the last 10 years, he and his wife, Dr. Barbara Laman, also an Emeritus English Professor of DSU, have resettled near family members in the Portland, OR, area. Between them, Dave and Barbara have five adult children and seven grandchildren.

Author photo courtesy of Barbara Laman.

About the Press

North Dakota State University Press (NDSU Press) exists to stimulate and coordinate interdisciplinary regional scholarship. These regions include the Red River Valley, the state of North Dakota, the plains of North America (comprising both the Great Plains of the United States and the prairies of Canada), and comparable regions of other continents. We publish peer reviewed regional scholarship shaped by national and international events and comparative studies.

Neither topic nor discipline limits the scope of NDSU Press publications. We consider manuscripts in any field of learning. We define our scope, however, by a regional focus in accord with the press's mission. Generally, works published by NDSU Press address regional life directly, as the subject of study. Such works contribute to scholarly knowledge of region (that is, discovery of new knowledge) or to public consciousness of region (that is, dissemination of information or interpretation of regional experience). Where regions abroad are treated, either for comparison or because of ties to those North American regions of primary concern to the press, the linkages are made plain. For nearly three-quarters of a century, NDSU Press has published substantial trade books, but the line of publications is not limited to that genre. We also publish textbooks (at any level), reference books, anthologies, reprints, papers, proceedings, and monographs. The press also considers works of poetry or fiction, provided they are established regional classics or they promise to assume landmark or reference status for the region. We select biographical or autobiographical works carefully for their prospective contribution to regional knowledge and culture. All publications, in whatever genre, are of such quality and substance as to embellish the imprint of NDSU Press.

Our name changed to North Dakota State University Press in January 2016. Prior to that, and since 1950, we published as the North Dakota Institute for Regional Studies Press. We continue to operate under the umbrella of the North Dakota Institute for Regional Studies, located at North Dakota State University.